Omar Vizquel

THE MAN WITH THE GOLDEN GLOVE

by
Dennis Manoloff

SPORTS PUBLISHING INC.
www.SportsPublishingInc.com

©1999 Sports Publishing Inc.
All rights reserved.

Production Manager: Susan M. McKinney
Cover design: Scot Muncaster
Photos: *The Associated Press,* Ben Vanhouten of the Seattle Mariners

ISBN: 1-58261-045-2
Library of Congress Catalog Card Number: 99-61954

SPORTS PUBLISHING INC.
sportspublishinginc.com

Printed in the United States.

CONTENTS

Omar Vizquel completes a double play in 1998 ALCS action against the Yankees. (AP/Wide World Photos)

1

The People's Ballplayer

The New York City subway regular is not easily amused or surprised. That is, until a major-league baseball player climbs aboard en route to Yankee Stadium for a playoff game.

At that moment, indifference gives way to shock.

About 4 p.m. on October 13, 1998, four hours before Game 6 of the American League Championship Series, Cleveland Indians shortstop Omar Vizquel dropped his token in the slot and waited for the No. 4 express from Grand Central Station, bound for the Bronx. Players and coaches from the visiting team typically ride a chartered bus to Yankee Stadium, or catch a taxi or limousine. They do not, as a rule, ride the subway, especially during the playoffs when Yankees fans are even more excited than usual.

Omar needed to get to work, however, and the subway had transported him to the stadium efficiently on certain occasions in the past. So he boarded the packed car and, one by one, newspapers and jaws dropped.

The whispers began. They soon became conversation. New Yorkers being New Yorkers, they did not keep it amongst themselves. They conversed with Omar, who happened to be a marked man. He had 10 hits in 20 at-bats in the first five games of the series.

If Omar was afraid of what the Yankees fans might say or do, he did not show it. He simply flashed his trademark smile and politely answered questions. "Some guys wished me luck; other guys told me I was going down," Omar told Liz Robbins of *The (Cleveland) Plain Dealer*. "It's really funny, the other side of the coin, what other people see."

During the brief walk to the stadium, Omar was followed by two men. They repeatedly asked if he was, indeed, Omar Vizquel, Indians short-stop. They would not take yes for an answer. Finally, when Omar walked into the players' entrance at the stadium, the two fans were convinced.

"That was him, wasn't it?" one said. "I thought it looked like him."

Omar laughed, wished them well and disappeared down the stairs. The people's ballplayer needed to get ready for a game.

From Caracas to Cleveland

Growing up in Caracas, Venezuela, Omar kicked a soccer ball before he threw a baseball. He was small and quick and liked to run, attributes ideal for soccer. Omar and his friends played on small fields, often the size of a basketball court, or on the basketball courts themselves.

Soccer developed his quick feet, which is a principle reason for his success in baseball. "If you're going to play the infield, you need to have good footwork," he said. "Your feet and your legs are the start of good defense." Omar also played basket-

*Growing up in Venezuela, Omar dreamed of making it
to the major leagues. (Seattle Mariners)*

ball and volleyball, which helped develop his hand-eye coordination.

The other sports were fun, but baseball was his game. His father, Omar, played at the semipro level in Venezuela. The elder Vizquel began working with his son when Omar was eight years old. By the time he was 14, Omar had made baseball a priority. Omar also looked up to Venezuelan major-league shortstops Luis Aparicio and Dave Concepcion, who were idolized by countless other youngsters in the country. At his first pro tryout, Omar remembered there being four third basemen, four second basemen, three first basemen and 15 shortstops.

Omar dreamed about following Concepcion and Aparicio to the majors, but reality was not as inviting. He faced long odds because of his diminutive stature. During the tryout, Omar was told he might want to try another sport. "One of the coaches took a look at me and said, 'You should go to the racetrack and be a jockey, because you're too small to play baseball,'" Omar told Paul Hoynes of *The Plain Dealer.* "That really made me mad. He had a shortstop in camp that he really liked. He gave him all the playing time while I sat on the bench. But I told him, 'The only thing that counts is what you do when you get to the United States.'"

Omar eventually grew to be 5-9 and 170 pounds, small by major-league standards. Regardless, he has been in the majors for 10 years. "Now, whenever I go home, I see that coach," Omar said. "I walk right next to him and laugh."

The road to the majors proved anything but smooth for Omar. He signed with the Seattle Mariners at the age of 16, which was cause for celebration. However, it took five long years for him to reach Seattle. During that time there were questions about whether he could hit. In 1985, he bat-

Omar made his major-league debut on April 3, 1989.
(Seattle Mariners)

ted .225 in 50 games for a lower-level team in the Mariners system. The next year, he batted .213 in 105 games for a different lower-level team. His glove kept the Mariners interested. Easing the sting of the .213 average, Omar led his league in fielding percentage at shortstop. Gradually, he became good enough at the plate to support his defense at the major-league level.

Omar made his major-league debut as the Mariners' Opening Day shortstop, April 3, 1989. Three days later, he singled off Storm Davis at Oakland for his first hit. Among other highlights that year was his first homer, on July 23, off Jimmy Key of the Blue Jays. Unfortunately, there were not enough other hits to make Omar happy. He batted .220 in 143 games.

After struggling at the plate two more seasons, Omar broke loose in 1992. In 136 games for the Mariners, he batted .294, the highest average among American League shortstops. As usual, his fielding was terrific. He led all major-league short-stops with a .989 fielding percentage, the seventh-best single-season mark in history. The Mariners stumbled to a 64-98 record, but Omar had proven he could field and hit in the majors. Any doubts about his ability were erased.

Omar batted .255 in 1993 and hit his first grand slam. More importantly, he won his first Gold Glove, awarded to the top defensive player at each position in each league. Watching from afar, Cleveland Indians General Manager John Hart liked what he saw, especially Omar's defensive skills. On December 20, Hart traded shortstop Felix Fermin and infielder Reggie Jefferson and cash to the Mariners for Omar. The Mariners appreciated Omar, but were reportedly cutting payroll.

Omar enjoyed playing for the Mariners and was sad to leave the team and the city, but looked forward to a new challenge. Hart assured Indians' fans that they would like their new shortstop. Yet even Hart had no idea that the city of Cleveland was about to embrace Omar as one of its own.

CHAPTER THREE

Giving Back to the Community

If Omar did nothing but play baseball and go home, the Indians would be satisfied. They would be appreciative of his unbelievable defense, solid offense and clubhouse leadership. But the Indians received more than a ballplayer when they acquired Omar from Seattle. They received a man who considers it a privilege to put on the uniform each day. As a result, Omar always seeks to give back to the community. "Omar loves people," said Allen Davis, director of community relations for the Indians. "It's genuine. It's

Omar takes time to talk to young fans. (Seattle Mariners)

not an act." Davis assists players with their personal appearances. His phone does not stop ringing with requests for Omar. "He's one of the few guys who keeps a calendar in his locker," Davis told Steve Herrick of *Indians Game Face* magazine. "He writes all of his appearances down. He has a very strong sense of responsibility. He takes it very seriously."

Omar does not pick and choose interaction with fans based on his mood.

"We had a commitment once during the playoffs," Davis said. "There was a night game the day before. It went late and we lost. I told him to meet me in the parking lot at Jacobs Field at 10:30 a.m. Omar was there. He looked so tired. He was walking and hobbling like an old man. But he kept his commitment. That's the kind of guy he is. He keeps his word."

Children occupy a particularly large spot in Omar's heart. Partly because of his size, but mostly because of his gentle nature, children are not intimidated by him. He regularly visits hospitals and lends his name and time to fund-raisers for education or arts programs. He even co-hosts, along with Davis, a show called "Omar y Amigos" — Omar and Friends—before Saturday home games. Children are invited to ask questions of Omar and a teammate; the show is aired on the scoreboard TV the next day.

Omar doesn't just bring the teammate with him on the show. He researches the player's statistics and highlights so he can tell the kids about them. Sometimes he gets humbled by a member of his audience. "One kid asked me, 'Who are you, and how many home runs have you hit?' " Omar said. Davis used to provide him with a script, but the shortstop was having too much fun to follow it.

Now the show goes wherever Omar takes it.

Omar actually enjoys signing autographs, even if it means his wrist hurts afterwards. When rows and rows of fans are packed against the railing down the third-base line in Jacobs Field, it can only mean Omar is signing.

Away from the ballpark, Omar autographs more than baseball-related items. An artist, Omar has become more and more serious about his paintings. A reproduction of one appears on Omar Vizquel Salsa, which debuted in 1998. A player is beyond popular when he gets his own salsa.

As recognizable as he is in Cleveland and other major-league cities, it barely compares to the buzz that occurs on trips home to Venezuela. Omar and Andres Galarraga, a Venezuelan who plays for the Braves, are the subject of kids' dreams. They are much like Aparicio and Concepcion were for Omar, who wears Concepcion's uniform number, 13.

Omar always wants to take care of the fans, but they never come before his family. He stays in constant touch with his mother and father, who live in Venezuela. He is married to Nicole; they have a son, Nico. It is common to see Omar in the clubhouse playing games with Nico.

Given all the attention he receives in both countries, Omar easily could begin to brag about himself. He could listen to everyone tell him how much they like him and say, "They're right. I am a great player." Or he could get tired of the attention and tell people to leave him alone. Omar would never think of it. The people close to him all make the same observation: Success has not changed him. In fact, Omar appreciates his place in baseball that much more. "My parents taught me to be grateful," he said.

CHAPTER FOUR

A New City

Almost from the moment he put on his Indians uniform, Omar generated excitement. Seattle fans had watched him begin to establish himself as a major leaguer. Cleveland fans, however, got to watch him blossom into an All-Star, on and off the field. The first game Omar played for the Indians came in their new ballpark, Jacobs Field. The Indians hoped their losing ways would finally end once they moved out of aging Municipal Stadium into a facility that was much more attractive to players and fans.

Omar stole a career-high 43 bases in 1997.
(AP/Wide World Photos)

Omar, known for his defensive play, has won six straight Gold Glove Awards. (AP/Wide World Photos)

"The park is beautiful," Omar said. "The infield is soft and the bounces are good, just the way I like it."

Opening Day 1994 was a festive occasion in Cleveland. It so happened that the Indians played Omar's former team, the Mariners. "It was strange," he said. The Indians won the game in extra innings. Three days later, Omar registered the first stolen base in Jacobs Field.

For the first time in his major-league career, Omar was playing for a legitimate playoff contender. Unfortunately, he was forced to watch from the sidelines for two months as the Indians battled the Chicago White Sox for first place in the American League Central Division. On April 22 at Texas, Rangers catcher Ivan Rodriguez slid hard into Omar on a play at second base. The Tribe's shortstop crashed to the ground in a heap and everyone in Cleveland feared the worst. It turned out that

Omar suffered a slight tear in a ligament in his right knee.

In late August, the Indians trailed the White Sox by one game when a labor dispute between baseball's owners and players ended the season. It did not resume, canceling the playoffs and World Series. Omar had been cheated out of his first chance at the postseason, but all was not lost. He finished with a modest .273 average, but batted .369 with runners in scoring position, the sixth-highest mark in the league. And he won his second consecutive Gold Glove, the first Indians shortstop ever to win the award.

He had a 51-game errorless streak as Indians fans got their first extended look at his defensive brilliance. They also watched a player who loved the game, a player who never bragged when he did well or made excuses when he struggled. As bitter as Indians fans were about the baseball strike, at least they had Omar and a superior team to keep them excited about the future.

Omar tries to stay warm during an April game in Cleveland. (AP/Wide World Photos)

CHAPTER FIVE

Keeping it Fun

Omar had fun playing baseball as a youngster. He sees no reason to change his approach just because he gets paid a lot of money. He views it as a game, not a chore.

Nobody enjoys playing baseball more than Omar. He never seems to stop smiling or laughing, from the moment he arrives at the park to the moment he leaves. Many players laugh and joke hours before a game, but get tense and grit their teeth as the first pitch approaches. Not Omar. He is always loose, especially between innings, no matter the opponent or the score. Omar uses this time to be creative.

While the pitcher throws his warm-ups, the infielders field a couple of routine ground balls thrown by the first baseman. When Indians first baseman Jim Thome throws in the shortstop's direction, no one knows what will happen next. Will Omar pull his glove back at the last second and let the ball roll up his foot, then kick it into his hand and fire back to Thome? Or will he turn his back to Thome's grounder and still catch the ball, sometimes between his legs? Occasionally he fields the ball normally but shocks Thome by firing a grounder back to first. It is Omar's way of "spicing up" the game.

Fans at any ballpark are advised to stay alert for what Omar might decide to do, like those in Kansas City during a game in September 1997. Between innings, the big-screen TV on the

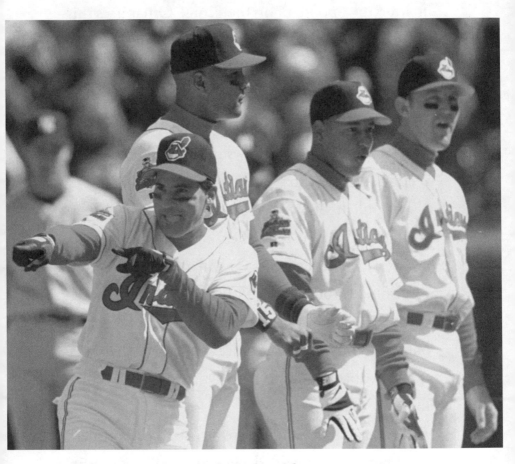

Omar, shown here at the Indians' home opener in 1996, is famous for his antics on the field and between innings. (AP/Wide World Photos)

scoreboard showed an imaginary line where fans could do the "limbo" and pretend to slide under it. Omar noticed the screen and began to do the limbo as he fielded a ground ball. A camera spotted him and flashed his moves on the screen. The crowd roared its approval.

When the pitcher completes his warm-ups and the game resumes, Omar continues to search for ways to make his job interesting. Over the years, he has taken the boredom out of a pop-up.

If the ball is hit into the outfield, he might catch it with his back to the plate and his glove at his waist, basket-style. If it is hit directly above him, he might catch the ball behind his head and then pull his arms apart rapidly, as if he were a Venus Fly Trap capturing an insect. Or he might use the one-handed snatch-catch, yanking the glove down sharply to his side, then flipping the ball behind him and gathering it with his bare hand.

The shows between innings, interaction with fans and stylish catches are all symbolic of a player thoroughly enjoying what he does. But it is a mistake to think Omar is some kind of class clown, the guy who goofs off all the time and pays no attention to the lesson being taught.

Behind the laughter and the flash is a player who takes his job very seriously. Omar can afford to be creative in the field only because he is a terrific defensive player. If he were not so gifted with the glove, he would never even attempt a Venus Fly Trap. Otherwise, he would probably drop the ball, get booed and be labeled a "hot dog." Omar is no hot dog. His six straight Gold Gloves give him license to bend the rules whenever he feels like it. "I want to make it interesting on things like pop-ups," Omar said. "But you have to make sure you catch the ball."

During a game, Omar occasionally will joke with teammates in the dugout when the Indians are batting. Sometimes he shares a laugh with the opposing catcher or one of the umpires. It is all part of Omar's attempt to have fun in what can be a very demanding and stressful game. Because Omar plays so relaxed, it can give the impression that he might not care about winning as much as others. Nothing could be further from the truth.

Omar does everything possible to help his team be successful. He never hesitates to dive for balls or slide head-first on a close play. "I don't let anything get in the way of trying to win," he said. "The most important thing is for my team to win games. It's no fun when you lose."

Since Omar was traded to Cleveland, the Indians have put together one of the winningest stretches in their history. The have won four Central Division titles and two American League

Omar has been to the World Series twice with the Indians. (AP/Wide World Photos)

Championships in the last four years. In 1995 the Indians played in the World Series for the first time since 1954. In 1997 they reached the World Series again, marking the first time in franchise history the Indians had reached the World Series two times in a three-year span. Omar has been synonymous with winning in Cleveland.

Reaching the Playoffs

When Major League Baseball finally resumed after the 1994 strike, Omar wished it could have waited one more day. In the Indians' 1995 opener, April 27 at Texas, he made two errors. A lesser fielder than Omar would have panicked; he used it as motivation. Omar made just seven errors in the next 135 games to end the season with a .986 fielding percentage, which earned him a third consecutive Gold Glove. At the plate, Omar batted .266 but had career bests in runs (87), hits (144), stolen bases (29), runs batted in (56),

Omar tags out Larry Sutton of the Royals during a rundown. (AP/Wide World Photos)

and home runs (six). His previous best season for homers was two.

Omar recorded another career-high that had nothing to do with offense or defense. For the first time in his career, he was ejected from a game. On August 11 at New York, he argued balls and strikes with plate umpire Derryl Cousins. Players can argue about a lot of issues with umpires, but not balls and strikes. Even one of the nicest players in baseball will be thrown out for that.

When the ejection happened, Omar's teammates were so shocked, they didn't know what to do. Some laughed, but made certain not to let Omar see them until he had calmed down. Sooner or later—probably sooner—they knew Omar was going to laugh it off himself. Regardless, he did make it clear that nice guys get mad, too.

Omar was one of many superb players on the Indians in 1995. As well as he performed during

Omar and teammate Kenny Lofton hug after clinching the American League Central Division title. (AP/Wide World Photos)

the regular season, he almost got lost among team-mates that included Albert Belle, Kenny Lofton, Carlos Baerga, Jim Thome, Manny Ramirez and Sandy Alomar Jr. They created an offensive ma-chine. Combined with quality starting pitching and a good bullpen, the Indians won 100 games and lost 44. It was the best record in the majors. They won the Central Division by 30 games and reached the playoffs for the first time in 41 years.

The city of Cleveland, which had almost given up on its baseball team ever making the playoffs again, turned the summer into one long party. Omar, who feeds off the energy of the fans, was having the time of his life. At least once a day it seemed Omar would stop and say, "Amazing. This is amazing."

In the first round of the playoffs, the Indians swept the Boston Red Sox, 3-0. Omar had two hits in 12 at-bats, but both of the hits were huge.

In the fifth inning of Game 2, he doubled to center to drive in two runs and give the Indians a 2-0 lead. They went on to win, 4-0. "I think that was the most important hit of my career," Omar said. Two days later, the Indians eliminated the Red Sox, 8-2, in Fenway Park. With the Indians leading, 5-1, in the sixth, Omar put away the Red Sox by smashing a two-out, two-run single.

Of course, Omar made several superb defensive plays as well. The best came when he changed direction and scooped up a ball that deflected off pitcher Charles Nagy's leg, throwing out the runner easily. When asked after the game how he makes so many difficult plays look so easy, Omar shook his head. "I don't know," he said. "I just look at the ball and, well, it happens sometimes. You have to concentrate."

As fate would have it, the Indians advanced to play the Mariners in the American League Championship Series. Omar was playing against his former teammates and friends for the right to go to the World Series. By the time the ALCS ended, the Mariners had seen enough of Omar. He did not hit much (2 for 23), but again dazzled with his glove.

In Game 2 at Seattle, he made two sensational plays as the Indians evened the series with a 5-2 victory. Omar used his knowledge of Mariners' hitters and the surroundings of the Kingdome to his advantage, positioning himself perfectly for numerous grounders. "I rely a lot on scouting reports, but it helped that I played there," he said.

Omar's defense was like cloud cover in Seattle. The Mariners and their fans knew it was coming, but were powerless to stop it. "He is as good as there is," Mariners manager Lou Piniella said. "He is the glue to their infield. He makes all the plays, and more. As a pitcher, you have to feel comfortable with him out there."

The Indians fell behind in the series, 2-1, but won the next three games. On October 17 in Seattle, they beat Randy Johnson, 4-0, to advance to the World Series. Omar's career had taken an interesting turn. He clinched his first World Series appearance by beating the team that had orginally signed him .

Because Game 6 concluded in the evening on the West Coast, the Indians' plane did not arrive in Cleveland until very early the next morning. That did not prevent thousands of Indians fans from coming out on a work day and greeting the players and coaches. It was a sight to behold, pure adrenaline from people of all ages. There was constant noise. Among the screams: "We love you, Omar!" As a little boy in Venezuela, he could not even have dreamed of something like this.

Unfortunately for Omar and the Indians, there were no more airport festivals, because the Atlanta

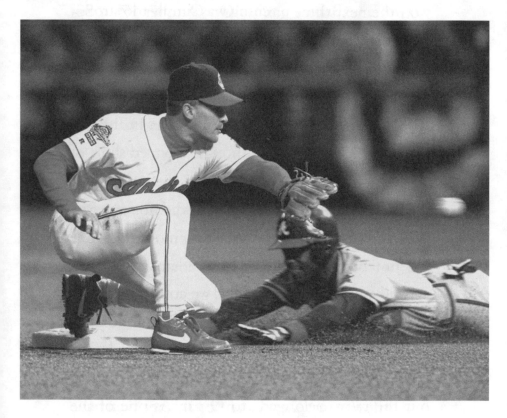

Omar and the Indians were disappointed when they lost the 1995 World Series to the Atlanta Braves, four games to two. (AP/Wide World Photos)

Braves beat them in the World Series, four games to two. The Braves' pitching was simply too strong, especially in Game 6, when Tom Glavine and Mark Wohlers held the Indians to one hit in a 1-0 victory at Atlanta.

One of the most incredible seasons in Indians history had ended. Even though it ended short of a championship, Omar refused to view the result as a disappointment. "No one wants to accept losing, but we had such a great season," he said. "There were a few guys crying and stuff, but I think everybody was happy with what we accomplished."

Before Cleveland drew the curtain on the 1995 Indians, the city held a downtown rally to honor them. Most of the players and coaches attended, but the rally belonged to Omar. As one of the players who spoke to an estimated 30,000 people, Omar had them laughing so hard they cried by cracking jokes in a routine worthy of a stand-up

Omar sits in the clubhouse at Yankee Stadium after the Indians' disappointing loss to the Yankees in the 1998 ALCS. (AP/Wide World Photos)

comedian. Before leaving the podium, Omar leaned into the microphone, waited for the shouts to quiet and yelled, "I love you, Cleveland!"

The 30,000 fans went wild. Omar, always popular, officially became part of the city's soul at that moment.

Fighting Through Injury

After the 1995 season, the Indians rewarded Omar with a six-year, $18-million contract (with a club option for a seventh year), the longest guaranteed contract in recent team history. It showed that you don't have to bat .320 or hit 40 homers to be appreciated. Omar could not wait to prove that the Indians were correct to have placed so much faith in him.

However, before the 1996 season began, he injured his right shoulder. He hoped the pain would go away by the end of spring training, but it did not. The shoulder got bad enough that Omar knew it eventually would need to be repaired. He could have had the surgery in the spring and missed a large portion of the season, but he did not want to let down his teammates, who counted on him.

The Indians had been in the World Series the previous year, and everyone was looking forward to another banner season. So Omar decided to postpone the surgery and play in pain.

His fielding suffered. Forced into hurrying his throws to try to compensate for the sore arm, Omar made 20 errors, the most in any season in his career. He had a legitimate excuse for the breakdown, but he would not use it. He never whined or complained. He rarely asked for a day off.

As painful as the experience was, Omar still maintained his sense of humor. When asked in midseason how he was treating his shoulder, he said,

"Now I'm using everything— ice, lotions, electricity, baby oil and guacamole sauce."

Even with the uncharacteristic errors, Omar made plenty of great plays in the field. The errors did not look so bad next to his offense. He established a career high in average (.297), and runs batted in (64) and stole 35 bases. He hit a career-high nine homers, including a grand slam. Perhaps most impressive, he played 151 games with a shoulder that felt like it was going to fall off each time he threw the ball. Omar didn't have to prove his toughness, but his teammates appreciated it. The Indians won 99 games and made the playoffs two consecutive years for the first time in franchise history. It took Omar's mind off his shoulder.

Entering the playoffs, Omar and the Indians were intent on winning the World Series this time. The Baltimore Orioles had other plans. The Orioles beat the Indians in the divisional series, three games to one. Before the playoffs really got started, they were over in Cleveland. There would be no downtown rally.

Despite the down year defensively, Omar earned another Gold Glove. He also won the Hutch Award, given annually to the major-league player who best exemplifies the character, desire and fighting spirit of Fred Hutchinson, the former Cincinnati Reds manager who died of cancer in 1964.

"I'm really proud of the way I played that year," Omar said. "It shows you how much I like the game. Some people overlook that."

Hart did not.

"Omar showed a lot of character," Hart said. "He played all year with a torn labrum and didn't blink. And he did it at a position where you've got to have a good arm."

In October, Omar underwent surgery. He did not get to enjoy a healthy shoulder again until early the next season.

Another Memorable Season

O nce again able to throw without discomfort, Omar cut his errors in half from the previous year and won his fifth consecutive Gold Glove in 1997. Omar did not make an error in his last 36 games of the regular season.

He added another solid season offensively as well, batting .280 with 89 runs, six triples and a career-high 43 steals in 55 attempts. He was the fourth-hardest player to strike out in the American League (one in 11.1 plate appearances) and led the league with 16 sacrifice bunts.

Omar didn't commit any errors during the division series against the Yankees in 1997. (AP/Wide World Photos)

All of the individual accomplishments would have been fruitless if the Indians could not make up for the playoff disappointment of 1996. Their victory total dropped to 86, but they still methodically won their third Central Division title in as many years.

In the first playoff round, the Indians faced the defending World Series champion New York Yankees. Cleveland fans treated the division series like a World Series because it was against the Yankees, who had given the Indians fits for decades.

The series turned out to be a classic, and Omar was in the middle of everything. With the Indians four outs from elimination in Game 4, Sandy Alomar Jr. homered to tie it. In the ninth, Omar singled off pitcher Ramiro Mendoza's body to drive in Marquis Grissom with the winning run. The deciding Game 5 was played the next night, and Omar responded. He completed a nifty double play in the second inning to help the Indians escape a jam. They went on to send home the Yankees with a dramatic 4-3 triumph. Omar played errorless defense in the series and had a team-high nine hits in 18 at-bats with four steals.

With the Yankees out of the way, the Indians got their chance for revenge. They faced the Orioles in the ALCS. Omar finished with one hit in 25 at-bats, but nonetheless figured in the the most important play of the series.

In the 12th inning of Game 3, he attempted a squeeze bunt with Grissom at third. Normally an excellent bunter, Omar missed the pitch and the ball got away from the catcher. Grissom scored to give the Indians a 2-1 victory. The Orioles argued that Omar fouled off the pitch and, therefore, the run should not have scored. At least one Oriole, catcher Lenny Webster, claimed that Omar later admitted that he tipped the ball. If Omar thought so, he never said so publicly. "I missed it," he said a thousand times. It was the best Omar ever felt about not doing his job correctly. The victory gave the Indians a 2-1 lead in the series, which they eventually won in six games.

In the 1995 World Series, Omar said the Braves taught the Indians how to lose. He hoped his team would do the same thing in the 1997 World Series to the Florida Marlins, who were making their first appearance in the fall classic.

The Indians came painfully close, leading 2-1 in the ninth inning of Game 7. They were two outs from their first world title since 1948. But the Marlins rallied to tie the game and won it two innings later. Omar and his teammates did not know what to think or feel. "Disbelief" was the word Omar used. "We were right there," he said.

If the Indians had won, Omar's defensive play in Game 6 would have been talked about forever in

Cleveland. With Marlins' runners on second and third and the Indians protecting a 4-1 lead in the sixth inning, he made a full-extension dive into the hole to snare a smash by catcher Charles Johnson. Omar skidded into the outfield grass, sprung to his feet and threw out Johnson by a step. The game ended, 4-1, because of Omar's magnificence.

"The most important play of my career," Omar said.

"Absolutely awesome," Thome said.

Immediately after that game, major media outlets such as ESPN, Fox, CNN and CNBC wanted interviews with Omar, who did his best to satisfy everybody. One Cleveland tv reporter kissed his glove. Omar rarely, if ever, congratulates himself. He allowed it to happen that night, searching for a tv replay of the Johnson highlight hours later. "I just wish that game could have been Game 7," he told his friends.

As happened in 1995, the city of Cleveland held a rally to honor the Indians for their memorable 1997 season. Another huge crowd showed up to cheer many of the players and coaches. The mood was upbeat, except the festivities lacked something: the presence of Omar. He still loved the city. He still loved his teammates and was proud of the Indians accomplishments, but he could not get the World Series loss out of his mind.

"I was depressed," he said. "I didn't want to be at the parade and have to put on a happy face."

Instead, he boarded a plane and hid in the Amazon. "I needed to get away from people and be around animals," he said. "And lagoons and waterfalls." Omar roamed a remote section of the Amazon.

He wanted to see an anaconda, but had to settle for tarantulas, macaws and green parrots. And Chief Wahoo, the symbol of the Indians. "One day in the middle of the jungle, there were some Americans, maybe 20 of them, with two guides," he said. "One of them had on an Indians cap. I couldn't believe it. It's not what you expect in the Amazon."

CHAPTER NINE

Omar the All-Star

In late June 1998, Omar said he would trade a potential sixth consecutive Gold Glove for an All-Star selection. For all his achievements in baseball, he never had been an All-Star. "It's hard for me to compete with guys who hit a lot of home runs," he said. "Obviously, defensive numbers don't count for a thing in this type of show."

Several days later, that changed. Indians manager Mike Hargrove named Omar as an American League reserve. Hargrove was the team's manager

Omar's 1998 fielding percentage was .993. (AP/Wide World Photos)

because the Indians were defending American League champions, but he did not need to apologize for picking his player over other deserving candidates. "He's having an All-Star season," Hargrove said.

Omar did not have to relinquish the Gold Glove to get there.

On May 12 at Tampa Bay, Omar failed to catch a simple flip from second baseman David Bell on a potential double-play ball, snapping a streak of 70 games without an error. It was the fourth-longest errorless streak by a shortstop in major-league history. "Stupid," Vizquel said. "I never thought it would end on a stupid play like that."

No matter. His colleagues did not think he was any less incredible with the leather. At one point in July, Omar had committed one error in 125 games, dating to the previous season. He finished 1998 with five errors and a fielding percentage of .993, sec-

Omar gets ready to exchange high fives with teammates Richie Sexson and Travis Fryman. (AP/Wide World Photos)

ond-best all-time among shortstops behind Cal Ripken Jr. (.996 in 1990).

"He's the best shortstop defensively I've ever seen, and I've seen some of the best in my lifetime," said Indians third baseman Travis Fryman, who once played in Detroit with Alan Trammell.

If Omar had been hitting .200 at the time of the All-Star selections, Hargrove probably would have bypassed him. But Omar was batting near .300 at that point in the year and he finished with a .288 average, 166 hits, 86 runs and 37 stolen bases.

For the fourth straight year, the Indians won the Central Division. They faced the Red Sox in the division series and beat them in four games. It set up another showdown with the Yankees, who had won an American League-record 114 games in the regular season. The Yankees were itching for revenge after what happened to them in the 1997 division series. The underdog Indians took a 2-1 lead in the ALCS, but the Yankees stormed back to win the next three games to advance to the World Series, where they swept the San Diego Padres, 4-0.

In the late innings of ALCS Game 6, Omar made the first error of his postseason career. It came on a wild throw and proved costly in a defeat. After the game, as the Indians packed up the season, Omar could not enjoy the fact that he was a team-best 11-of-25 against the Yankees in the series. "This hurts," he said. "It's like someone stuck a knife in your heart." Omar and many of his teammates wondered if a World Series title would ever be theirs.

CHAPTER TEN

Defense, Defense, Defense

Omar was not born with a glove on his left hand. It only seems that way.

Entering his 11th season in the majors in 1999, Omar is recognized as one of the best defensive players ever at his position. Last year he earned his sixth consecutive Gold Glove. He ranks fourth all-time among Gold Glove recipients at shortstop, behind Ozzie Smith (13), Aparicio (9), and Mark Belanger (8). Omar finished the 1998 season as the all-time leader in fielding percentage among shortstops with at least 1,000 games (.982).

Omar works hard at being a good defensive shortstop.
(AP/Wide World Photos)

The Gold Gloves and the amazing statistics only begin to measure Omar's defensive genius. What separates him from the rest is a knack for making fielding an art form. He has earned the nickname "Maestro," for the way he orchestrates the Indians' defense. His teammates look up to him as the conductor because no matter how many times the ball is hit to him, Omar gives the impression that everything is under control.

If Omar isn't worried, why should anyone else be? He wants balls hit to him, the more difficult the better. He loves to make the sensational plays, and he makes them look easy. Dives to his right. Dives to his left. Backhands on the run. Split-legged leaps over runners to turn double plays. And, of course, the barehand grab.

Mark McGwire and Sammy Sosa have their homers. Randy Johnson and Roger Clemens have their strikeouts. Omar has his barehand grabs, the infielder's equivalent of walking a tightrope without a net. The undisputed king of the barehand, he uses it more in one season than many players do in a career. Omar insists he is not trying to show off, or to show-up the opponent. "I use the barehand when I think it is necessary to get the guy out," he said. "I don't think about it. It's a reaction play."

Perhaps his most dramatic, and daring, barehand occurred April 22, 1993, against Boston in the Kingdome. He fielded a chopper off the bat of Ernest Riles and got him for the final out of a no-hitter by Chris Bosio.

Because Omar makes so many spectacular plays, it is possible to forget that he makes all the routine ones, as well. He knows that before you can apply the frosting, you need to bake the cake.

"Omar pays attention to the fundamentals," said Johnny Goryl, former infield coach of the Indians. "He knows how to play the position. He knows exactly what he's doing."

Omar does not just put on his glove and hope to make plays. Before taking the field, he studies videos and charts of other team's batters to get a feel for where they hit the ball, or he relies on his memory of previous games. He combines that information with his knowledge of the Indians pitchers to give him a good idea where to position himself for each batter.

During the game, Omar adjusts that positioning based on little things he picks up from the batters and pitchers. A right-handed batter might have changed his stance and approach because two runners are on instead of none, and the Indians pitcher might be getting tired, meaning his pitches aren't as sharp and are easier to pull. So Omar might move a few steps deeper and into the hole more than he planned.

The adjustments happen all the time, which is why Omar rarely looks surprised by anything that happens on the field. "Omar is one of the smartest guys in the game," said Buddy Bell, former infield coach of the Indians.

The intelligence would not amount to much without help from his body. Omar uses his cat-quick feet to pounce on balls in any direction. "His balance is tremendous," Goryl said. "Even when it looks like he should be off-balance he isn't, because he is so agile."

As the pitch is being made, Omar starts moving and never gets caught flat-footed. Then he turns it over to his soft hands and his small glove. "He has the best set of hands I've seen in a long time," said former teammate Tony Fernandez, a splendid defensive player in his own right.

None of it happens by accident. Omar possesses plenty of natural ability, but he did not become an adept fielder by playing video games in the living room. "You have to work hard every year," he said. "You can't take anything for granted."

Besides a World Series ring, Omar has one other major goal. "I want to go through a season without making an error," he said.

He just might do it.

Omar Vizquel Quick Facts

Full Name:	Omar Enrique Vizquel
Team:	Cleveland Indians
Hometown:	Caracas, Venezuela
Position:	Shortstop
Jersey Number:	13
Bats:	Switch-hitter
Throws:	Right
Height:	5-9
Weight:	170 pounds
Birthdate:	April 24, 1967

1998 Highlight: Led all major league shortstops in fielding and was awarded his sixth consecutive Gold Glove award.

Stats Spotlight: His career fielding percentage (.982) is the best among shortstops in major league history.

Little-Known Fact: Omar is an avid painter and artist.

Omar Vizquel's Professional Career

Year	Club	AVG	G	AB	R	H	2B	3B	HR	RBI	BB	SO	SB
1989	Seattle	.220	143	387	45	85	7	3	1	20	28	40	1
1990	Seattle	.247	81	255	19	63	3	2	2	18	18	22	4
1991	Seattle	.230	142	426	42	98	16	4	1	41	45	37	7
1992	Seattle	.294	136	483	49	142	20	4	0	21	32	38	15
1993	Seattle	.255	158	560	68	143	14	2	2	31	50	71	12
1994	Cleveland	.273	69	286	39	78	10	1	1	33	23	23	13
1995	Cleveland	.266	136	542	87	144	28	0	6	56	59	59	29
1996	Cleveland	.297	151	542	98	161	36	1	9	64	56	42	35
1997	Cleveland	.280	153	565	89	158	23	6	5	49	57	58	43
1998	Cleveland	.288	151	576	86	166	30	6	2	50	62	64	37

Cleveland Totals		.268	1320	4622	622	1238	187	29	29	383	430	454	196
Post Season Ttls		.232	47	185	23	43	5	2	0	11	22	32	22

Career Fielding Statistics

Year	Team	Posn	G	GS	TC	PO	A	E	DP	FLD%
1989	Seattle	SS	143	131	614	208	388	18	102	.971
1990	Seattle	SS	81	78	349	103	239	7	48	.980
1991	Seattle	2B	1	0	0	0	0	0	0	—
1991	Seattle	SS	138	123	659	224	422	13	105	.980
1992	Seattle	SS	136	128	633	223	403	7	92	.989
1993	Seattle	SS	155	150	735	245	475	15	108	.980
1994	Cleveland	SS	69	68	323	113	204	6	54	.981
1995	Cleveland	SS	136	135	624	210	405	9	84	.986
1996	Cleveland	SS	150	149	693	226	447	20	91	.971
1997	Cleveland	SS	152	149	684	245	429	10	98	.985
1998	Cleveland	SS	151	149	720	273	442	5	94	.993

Fielding Totals			1312	1260	6034	2070	3854	110	876	.982
Post Season Fielding Ttls			47	47	238	85	152	1	39	.996

1998 AL Triples Leaders

Jose Offerman	13
Johnny Damon	10
Randy Winn	9
Ray Durham	8
Derek Jeter	8
Nomar Garciaparra	8
Troy O'Leary	8
Garret Anderson	7
Quinton McCracken	7
Joey Cora	6
Matt Lawton	6
Kenny Lofton	6
Mike Caruso	6
Otis Nixon	6
Omar Vizquel	**6**

1998 AL Stolen Base Leaders

Rickey Henderson	66
Kenny Lofton	54
Shannon Stewart	51
Alex Rodriguez	46
Jose Offerman	45
Brian Hunter	42
Tom Goodwin	38
Otis Nixon	37
Omar Vizquel	**37**
Ray Durham	36

Omar vs. MLB Starting Shortstops in 1998

Player	Fielding %
Omar Vizquel	**.993**
Mike Bordick	.990
Derek Jeter	.986
Deivi Cruz	.983
Gary Disarcina	.980
Chris Gomez	.980
Kevin Stocker	.979
Rich Aurilia	.979
Barry Larkin	.979
Ricky Gutierrez	.976
Alex Rodriguez	.976
Kevin Elster	.976
Alex Gonzalez	.976
Neifi Perez	.975

Rey Ordonez	.975
Royce Clayton	.971
Jay Bell	.971
Walt Weiss	.967
Pat Meares	.966
Edgar Renteria	.966
Jeff Blauser	.965
Jose Valentin	.963
Nomar Garciaparra	.962
Desi Relaford	.960
Lou Collier	.960
Mark Grudzielanek	.954
Miguel Tejada	.950
Mike Caruso	.944
Average	**.972**

***Omar makes one of his leaping throws to complete a double play.
(AP/Wide World Photos)***

Career Fielding Statistics of Hall of Fame SSs vs. Vizquel

Players	Team	G	PO	A	E	DP	FLD%
Luis Aparicio	Chi-Bal-Bos	2599	4548	8016	366	1553	.972
Luke Appling	Chi	2422	4674	7543	672	1477	.948
Lou Boudreau	Cle-Bos	1646	3265	4877	230	1205	.973
Pee Wee Reese	Bkn-LA	2166	4124	6131	407	1255	.962
Phil Rizzuto	NY	1661	3220	4666	263	1217	.968
Omar Vizquel	**Sea-Cle**	**1312**	**2070**	**3854**	**110**	**876**	**.982**

Omar Vizquel's
Career Highlights

1998:

- Led all major meague shortstops with a .993 fielding percentage, the second-highest single-season fielding percentage by a shortstop in history behind Cal Ripken's .996 in 1990. Omar's career fielding percentage of .982 is the highest figure in MLB history among shortstops with at least 1,000 games played at that position.

- His 70-game errorless streak in 1998 stands as the fourth-longest in MLB history by a shortstop.

- Awarded his sixth consecutive Gold Glove Award. He's now ranked fourth in all-time Gold Gloves.

- Was selected to the American League All-Star Team , marking the first time an Indian short-stop was an All-Star since Lou Boudreau in 1948.

- Omar hit a combined .300 (12 for 40) in 10 post-season games with a triple and three runs scored. Also stole a team-high four bases in five attempts.

1997:

- Swiped a career-best 43 bases in 55 attempts, the fifth-highest total in the American League.

- Won his fifth consecutive Gold Glove Award, committing only 10 errors in 683 total chances for a .985 fielding percentage.

- Collected his 1,000th career hit

- Was the fourth most difficult AL hitter to strike out (11.1 plate appearances per strikeout).

1996:

- Had career's best season from an offensive standpoint, collecting personal highs in almost every offensive category. Registered career-highs in runs (98), hits (161), batting average (.297), doubles (36), home runs (9), RBI (64) and steals (35).

- Was hitting .308 through September 15, but a six-for-39 slump over the last 11 games dropped his average to just under the .300 mark.

- Honored with Gold Glove Award for fourth straight year.

1995:

- Signed to a six-year contract by the Indians.
- Won his third consecutive Gold Glove Award. Had a 47-game errorless streak from June 12 to August 4.

- Was the second-most difficult player in the AL to double up, hitting into just four double plays all season.

- Finished fifth in the AL in both the categories of sacrifice hits and sacrifice flies.

1994:

- In his first season with Cleveland, he became the first Indians shortstop ever to win the Gold Glove Award. His .982 fielding percentage ranked third among AL shortstops. He made only three errors after April 16.

- On August 7 against Boston, he collected a career-high six RBI.

- Sat out games from April 24 through June 13 with a knee injury.

- Batted .369 with runners in scoring position, the sixth-best mark in the league.

1993:

- In his final season with the Seattle Mariners, he captured the Gold Glove Award for the first time in his career.

- Did not play on Aug. 18 at Baltimore, snapping a string of 214 consecutive games.

- In his 1,748th career plate appearance, he received the first intentional walk of his career.

- Bare-handing an Ernest Riles chopper, he recorded the final assist in Chris Bosio's no-hitter against the Red Sox.

1992:

- Led all Major League shortstops with a .989 fielding percentage, the seventh-best season average in ML history.

- Paced all AL shortstops with a .294 batting average, a mark 64 points higher than his '91 average.

- Had a career-best 14-game hitting streak for the Mariners in August.

1991:

- Went five-for-five on July 18th at Milwaukee, tying Mariners' record for hits in a game.

- Batted .312 with runners in scoring position.

1990:

- After sitting out the first half of the season with a knee injury, he was recalled to the Majors by the Mariners on July 5 and homered at Cleveland in his first game.

- Finished third among AL shortstops in fielding.

1989:

- Made his Major League debut as Mariners' opening day shortstop on April 3.

- Singled off Storm Davis on April 6 for his first big league hit.

- Hit first Major League home run off Jimmy Key of the Blue Jays on July 23.

Derek Jeter: The Yankee Kid

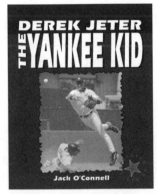

Author: Jack O'Connell
ISBN: 1-58261-043-6

In 1996 Derek burst onto the scene as one of the most promising young shortstops to hit the big leagues in a long time. His hitting prowess and ability to turn the double play have definitely fulfilled the early predictions of greatness.

A native of Kalamazoo, MI, Jeter has remained well grounded. He patiently signs autographs and takes time to talk to the young fans who will be eager to read more about him in this book.

Bernie Williams: Quiet Superstar

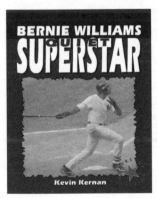

Author: Kevin Kernan
ISBN: 1-58261-044-4

Bernie Williams, a guitar-strumming native of Puerto Rico, is not only popular with his teammates, but is considered by top team officials to be the heir to DiMaggio and Mantle fame.

He draws frequent comparisons to Roberto Clemente, perhaps the greatest player ever from Puerto Rico. Like Clemente, Williams is humble, unassuming, and carries himself with quiet dignity. Also like Clemente, he plays with rare determination and a special elegance. He's married, and serves as a role model not only for his three children, but for his young fans here and in Puerto Rico.

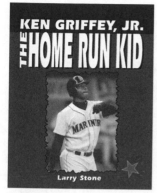

Ken Griffey, Jr.: The Home Run Kid

Author: Larry Stone
ISBN: 1-58261-041-x

Capable of hitting majestic home runs, making breathtaking catches, and speeding around the bases to beat the tag by a split second, Ken Griffey, Jr. is baseball's Michael Jordan. Amazingly, Ken reached the Major Leagues at age 19, made his first All-Star team at 20, and produced his first 100 RBI season at 21.

The son of Ken Griffey, Sr., Ken is part of the only father-son combination to play in the same outfield together in the same game, and, like Barry Bonds, he's a famous son who turned out to be a better player than his father.

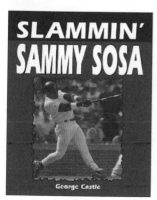

Sammy Sosa: Slammin' Sammy

Author: George Castle
ISBN: 1-58261-029-0

1998 was a break-out year for Sammy as he amassed 66 home runs, led the Chicago Cubs into the playoffs and finished the year with baseball's ultimate individual honor, MVP.

When the national spotlight was shone on Sammy during his home run chase with Mark McGwire, America got to see what a special person he is. His infectious good humor and kind heart have made him a role model across the country.

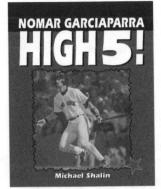

Nomar Garciaparra: High 5!
Author: Mike Shalin
ISBN: 1-58261-053-3

An All-American at Georgia Tech, a star on the 1992 U.S. Olympic Team, the twelfth overall pick in the 1994 draft, and the 1997 American League Rookie of the Year, Garciaparra has exemplified excellence on every level.

At shortstop, he'll glide deep into the hole, stab a sharply hit grounder, then throw out an opponent on the run. At the plate, he'll uncoil his body and deliver a clutch double or game-winning homer. Nomar is one of the game's most complete players.

Juan Gonzalez: Juan Gone!
Author: Evan Grant
ISBN: 1-58261-048-7

One of the most prodigious and feared sluggers in the major leagues, Gonzalez was a two-time home run king by the time he was 24 years old.

After having something of a personal crisis in 1996, the Puerto Rican redirected his priorities and now says baseball is the third most important thing in his life after God and family.

Mo Vaughn:
Angel on a Mission

Author: Mike Shalin
ISBN: 1-58261-046-0

Growing up in Connecticut, this Angels slugger learned the difference between right and wrong and the value of honesty and integrity from his parents early on, lessons that have stayed with him his whole life.

This former American League MVP was so active in Boston charities and youth programs that he quickly became one of the most popular players ever to don the Red Sox uniform.

Mo will be a welcome addition to the Angels line-up and the Anaheim community.

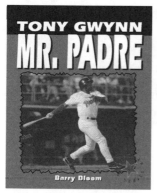

Tony Gwynn:
Mr. Padre

Author: Barry Bloom
ISBN: 1-58261-049-5

Tony is regarded as one of the greatest hitters of all-time. He is one of only three hitters in baseball history to win eight batting titles (the others: Ty Cobb and Honus Wagner).

In 1995 he won the Branch Rickey Award for Community Service by a major leaguer. He is unfailingly humble and always accessible, and he holds the game in deep respect. A throwback to an earlier era, Gwynn makes hitting look effortless, but no one works harder at his craft.

Sandy and Roberto Alomar: Baseball Brothers

Author: Barry Bloom
ISBN: 1-58261-054-1

Sandy and Roberto Alomar are not just famous baseball brothers they are also famous baseball sons. Sandy Alomar, Sr. played in the major leagues fourteen seasons and later went into management. His two baseball sons have made names for themselves and have appeared in multiple All-Star games.

With Roberto joining Sandy in Cleveland, the Indians look to be a front-running contender in the American League Central.

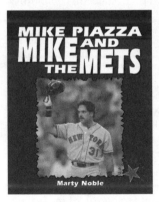

Mike Piazza: Mike and the Mets

Author: Marty Noble
ISBN: 1-58261-051-7

A total of 1,389 players were selected ahead of Mike Piazza in the 1988 draft, who wasn't picked until the 62nd round, and then only because Tommy Lasorda urged the Dodgers to take him as a favor to his friend Vince Piazza, Mike's father.

Named in the same breath with great catchers of another era like Bench, Dickey and Berra, Mike has proved the validity of his father's constant reminder "If you work hard, dreams do come true."

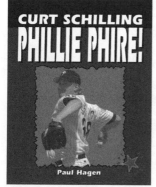

Curt Schilling: Phillie Phire!

Author: Paul Hagen
ISBN: 1-58261-055-x

Born in Anchorage, Alaska, Schilling has found a warm reception from the Philadelphia Phillies faithful. He has amassed 300+ strikeouts in the past two seasons and even holds the National League record for most strikeouts by a right handed pitcher at 319.

This book tells of the difficulties Curt faced being traded several times as a young player, and how he has been able to deal with off-the-field problems.

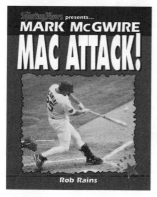

Mark McGwire: Mac Attack!

Author: Rob Rains
ISBN: 1-58261-004-5

Mac Attack! describes how McGwire overcame poor eyesight and various injuries to become one of the most revered hitters in baseball today. He quickly has become a legendary figure in St. Louis, the home to baseball legends such as Stan Musial, Lou Brock, Bob Gibson, Red Schoendienst and Ozzie Smith. McGwire thought about being a police officer growing up, but he hit a home run in his first Little League at-bat and the rest is history.

Roger Clemens: Rocket Man!

Author: Kevin Kernan
ISBN: 1-58261-128-9

Alex Rodriguez: A-plus Shortstop

ISBN: 1-58261-104-1

SUPERSTAR SERIES

Baseball
SuperStar Series Titles

Collect Them All!

____ Sandy and Roberto Alomar: Baseball Brothers

____ Kevin Brown: Kevin with a "K"

____ Roger Clemens: Rocket Man!

____ Juan Gonzalez: Juan Gone!

____ Mark Grace: Winning With Grace

____ Ken Griffey, Jr.: The Home Run Kid

____ Tony Gwynn: Mr. Padre

____ Derek Jeter: The Yankee Kid

____ Randy Johnson: Arizona Heat!

____ Pedro Martinez: Throwing Strikes

____ Mike Piazza: Mike and the Mets

____ Alex Rodriguez: A-plus Shortstop

____ Curt Schilling: Philly Phire!

____ Sammy Sosa: Slammin' Sammy

____ Mo Vaughn: Angel on a Mission

____ Omar Vizquel: The Man with a Golden Glove

____ Larry Walker: Colorado Hit Man!

____ Bernie Williams: Quiet Superstar

____ Mark McGwire: Mac Attack!

Available by calling 877-424-BOOK